BC ANF

GW00381669

FINGERFOOD

MORE THAN 80 STYLISH IDEAS

Withdrawn Stock
Dorset County Council

DORSET COUNTY LIBRARY

400 000 739 N

FINGERFOOD

MORE THAN 80 STYLISH IDEAS

Dorset County Library	
Askews & Holts	2011
641.812	£8.99

MURDOCH BOOKS

contents

nibbled No event is a true do without spectacular nibbles, but throwing together the ideal menu is about so much more than just cooking small. First and foremost it's about knowing what kind of party you want — from a sophisticated tea party to a glam evening of cocktails. Just add a little bit of planning and a good dash of inspiration for a fabulous occasion.

nibbled

The key elements to take into account when planning a menu of nibbles are the type of event you are catering for, the tastes of your guests and number of people you are expecting. To help with this we've divided this book into five chapters designed to reflect the five most common types of party at which you'd expect to serve nibbles: brunch, outdoor lunch, tea, cocktails and lounge. Each of these events is defined by both the time of day it is held and the kind of ambience you want to create.

Regular party goers fall into two key categories — those who see the food as the main event, and those who simply view it as a way to help the drinks go down. With a little bit of imagination, it's easy to plan a menu that caters for both of these groups and creates a cohesive mood. Whatever type of party you're holding, from breakfast through to a midnight feast, the cardinal rule is to make sure that there is enough food for everyone. Hungry guests can easily turn into beyond-tipsy guests. So don't even think about under-catering; plan to be super generous and then ramp up the quantities by another third. With this in mind, it's time to start planning an event that will live on in the memory of all those who are lucky enough to be invited.

The tastes, likes and dislikes of your guests should play an important role in your menu selection. If you're having a small party with close friends this shouldn't be hard to achieve, but if you are throwing a large bash or catering for someone else, you will need to include some variations. Vegetarian options are a must and you may also want to dish up some dairy-free and wheat-free nibbles as well as low-carb delicacies.

Numbers have a significant impact on the style and tone of any party and they'll certainly have an impact on the menu you select. The two main considerations are the amount of work required to prepare the food and any issues of presentation involved. It goes without saying that the more fiddly a dish is to prepare the harder it will be to make it in bulk. Not that this should be a reason to discount a delicacy that appeals to you — it simply requires a greater depth of planning. If you're hosting a major event with hordes of people, don't even consider trying to do it all yourself. The trick here is organization and delegation. Make sure you are clear on what kind of help you need and which tasks need to be completed in which order. Stock up on soft drinks, chips and dips for any willing helpers and get the party started in the kitchen.

While it can definitely be easier to cater for smaller numbers, different considerations come into play. At a crowded party it's fine to be dashing in and out of the kitchen, doing a little mingling, handing round a platter and generally flitting about. With a small gathering, though, the name of the game is intimacy and conversation, an atmosphere that is hard to create if you're squirreled away in the kitchen. Keeping this in mind, it's wise to create a menu that allows you to prepare as much as possible beforehand so that you are able to be both present and relaxed when guests arrive.

Although it is the quality and flavour of the food that your guests will appreciate the most, the way in which it is served can add glamour and verve to the simplest event. White platters are the standard fallback for serving nibbles for a good reason — they offer a neutral background that allows the food to stand out and are an easy way to create a simple and cohesive style. If, however, you are confident about experimenting with the food you serve, why not throw caution to the wind and experiment with the way in which you present it? Creating a look for your party is another tool in the quest to create atmosphere.

If you're catering for a crowd, put together a flotilla of hostess trolleys for a cute and easy way to serve mountains of food. Tea looks oh so pretty served on mismatched plates from delicate old dinner services. Head to your closest charity shop and put together a whole new look on a shoestring. If the food leans towards Asia, stock up on mini bamboo steamers as a cheap and funky way to dress up the food. And lastly, don't forget to turn to the outdoors for beautiful ways to dress up the food — flowers, twigs, leaves and stones all lend an uncontrived beauty to a plate of fabulous food.

Food, drinks, music, company and atmosphere are all important elements of any successful party. The most vital element, though, is you. While fabulous food will make your party memorable, the guests have come to see you and you'll miss all the fun if you're chained to the stove. If you're at all nervous about your catering abilities, start small and keep it simple. Stick to recipes you know or, if you must experiment, have a practice run first. If impact is essential, pull out all the stops, but don't try to do it on your own. The best way to ensure that a good time is had by all is to mix, mingle and flirt to the best of your ability.

champagne brunch   Pop open some bubbly, pile platters with goodies and start the weekend with a bang. Breakfast celebrations are a charming choice for a get-together. We're usually at our best mid-morning, so start at a civilized hour and get the party rolling. Sweets are always a winner, so are savouries — bubbly and brioche, salmon and salsa, fried eggs and fritters; mix up an eclectic feast.

Brunch has a rhythm all of its own. Some will have eaten already, others will wait, but either way you're free to indulge in some wilder flavours and combinations. The lunch element is what makes brunch so special: the combination of brekky treats and lunchtime delights allows for twice the grazing pleasure in one meal. It's important to assume that your guests might not have eaten yet. Empty stomachs demand special consideration in several different ways. Many of us are a little squeamish when it comes to the first meal of the day; make sure you offer a good selection of comfort food for those who find it hard to look a coffee in the face first thing. Serving drinks at an early hour can be a heady way to start the day so make sure you offer enough food to go around or things may get a little sticky. Going for an early rather than later party also gives you less time to prepare so figure this into your schedule when planning the menu. Brunch also allows you to experiment with drinks. Try toe-curlingly good bellinis, bucks fizz or kir royales, and whip up frothy, luscious smoothies for those who choose not to imbibe. Neither event would be complete without excellent-quality coffee and tea. If you don't have a coffee machine, now is the time to beg, borrow or steal one. Recruit a willing volunteer to man the machine and complement the delicious food with steaming hot drinks.

The earthy aroma of mushroom perfumes these dainty frittatas garnished with an elegant shaving of Parmesan.

mini mushroom frittatas

25 g (1 oz) butter
8 small Swiss brown mushrooms, cut into quarters
80 g (2¾ oz) very small button mushrooms
2 eggs
3 tablespoons cream
1 tablespoon plain (all-purpose) flour
1 tablespoon finely chopped chives
2 tablespoons finely chopped parsley
2 tablespoons grated Parmesan cheese
6 pieces shaved Parmesan cheese, to serve

Heat the butter in a small frying pan over medium heat. When sizzling, add the mushrooms and cook for 5 minutes. Remove and allow to cool.

Preheat the oven to 180°C (350°F/Gas 4) and generously grease six holes in a muffin tray.

In a bowl, combine the eggs, cream, flour, chives, parsley and Parmesan. Season well with salt and pepper. Stir in the mushrooms and spoon the mixture into the muffin holes. Bake for 15 minutes. Cool for 5 minutes before removing from the tray. Serve warm, garnished with a piece of shaved Parmesan.

Makes 6

mini mushroom frittatas

quail eggs with spiced salts

2 teaspoons cumin seeds
48 quail eggs
125 g (4$^{1}/_{2}$ oz/$^{1}/_{2}$ cup) good-
   quality table salt

1$^{1}/_{2}$ teaspoons five-spice powder
3 teaspoons celery salt

Toast the cumin seeds in a dry frying pan over low heat for 1–2 minutes, or until richly fragrant. Cool slightly, then grind to a fine powder.

Put half the eggs in a large saucepan of water, bring to the boil and cook for 1$^{1}/_{2}$ minutes for medium- to hard-boiled eggs. Remove from the pan and rinse under cold water to cool. Repeat with the remaining eggs.

Divide the table salt among three small bowls. Add the five-spice powder to one, the celery salt to another and the ground cumin to the third. Mix the flavourings into the salt.

To serve, pile the eggs into a large bowl and serve with the three bowls of spiced salts. Invite your guests to peel their own eggs, then dip them into the flavoured salt of their choice.

Makes 48

petit croque-monsieur

16 slices white bread
125 g (4 1/2 oz/1/2 cup)
    wholegrain mustard
100 g (3 1/2 oz) thinly shaved
    honey ham
100 g (3 1/2 oz) thinly sliced
    Jarlsberg cheese

55 g (2 oz/1/3 cup) very finely
    chopped mustard fruits
    (optional)
40 g (1 1/2 oz) butter
2 tablespoons olive oil

Spread each slice of bread with mustard. Lay out eight bread slices on a board, mustard-side-up, and top with the shaved ham, then the cheese slices. If you are using mustard fruits, sprinkle them over the cheese. Press the remaining bread slices on top, mustard-side-down, to make eight sandwiches. Trim off the crusts, then cut each sandwich into three fingers.

Melt half the butter and oil in a non-stick frying pan. When the butter begins to foam, cook half the fingers until crisp and golden on both sides and the cheese is just starting to melt. Remove and keep warm on a baking tray in the oven. Melt the remaining butter and oil in the frying pan and cook the remaining fingers. Serve warm.

Makes 24

quail eggs with spiced salts

petit croque-monsieur

corn and potato fritters

2 large potatoes
265 g (9^1/$_2$ oz/1^1/$_3$ cups) tinned
   corn kernels, drained
4 eggs, lightly beaten
6 spring onions (scallions),
   chopped
50 g (1^3/$_4$ oz/^{1}/$_2$ cup) dry
   breadcrumbs

1 teaspoon garam masala
3 tablespoons oil

dipping sauce

160 g (5^3/$_4$ oz/^{2}/$_3$ cup) plain
   yoghurt
2 tablespoons chopped mint
2 teaspoons sweet chilli sauce

Peel and coarsely grate the potatoes. Drain on paper towels and squeeze out the excess moisture. Combine in a bowl with the corn, eggs, spring onion, breadcrumbs and garam masala. Mix well.

To make the dipping sauce, combine all the ingredients in a bowl.

Heat 2 tablespoons of the oil in a heavy-based frying pan over medium heat. Cook heaped tablespoons of the mixture for 2 minutes on each side, or until golden. Drain on crumpled paper towels and keep warm. Repeat until all the mixture is used, adding extra oil to the frying pan if necessary. Serve with the dipping sauce.

Makes about 40

herb pancakes with avocado butter

60 g (2¹/₄ oz/¹/₂ cup) plain
   (all-purpose) flour
60 g (2¹/₄ oz/¹/₂ cup)
   self-raising flour
1 egg, lightly beaten
125 ml (4¹/₂ fl oz/¹/₂ cup) milk
4 tablespoons fresh mixed herbs
1 teaspoon cracked black pepper
melted butter, for pan-frying

2 tablespoons baby capers, fried

avocado butter
¹/₂ ripe avocado, mashed
60 g (2¹/₄ oz) butter, softened
1 tablespoon lemon or lime
   juice
¹/₂ teaspoon cracked black
   pepper

Sift the flours into a large bowl and make a well in the centre. Gradually add the combined egg, milk, herbs and pepper, whisking until the batter is smooth and free of lumps.

Heat a frying pan and brush with melted butter. Drop teaspoons of batter into the pan and cook until bubbles appear on top. Turn and cook until golden underneath. Keep warm.

To make the avocado butter, mix the ingredients together until smooth. Spread on top of the pancakes, garnish with the baby capers and serve.

Makes about 50

herb pancakes with avocado butter

Ideally suited to breakfast, polenta muffins make a warm and tasty base for the sublime mix of prawns and dill mayonnaise.

mini polenta muffins with prawns and dill mayonnaise

250 g (9 oz/2 cups) plain (all-purpose) flour, sifted
110 g (3^{3}/$_{4}$ oz/^{3}/$_{4}$ cup) polenta
1 tablespoon baking powder
55 g (2 oz/^{1}/$_{4}$ cup) sugar
2 eggs, lightly beaten
125 g (4^{1}/$_{2}$ oz) butter, melted
250 ml (9 fl oz/1 cup) milk
3 tablespoons finely chopped dill
1 tablespoon lemon juice
1 teaspoon horseradish cream
375 g (13 oz/1^{1}/$_{2}$ cups) whole-egg mayonnaise
30 small cooked prawns (shrimp)

Preheat the oven to 200°C (400°F/Gas 6) and lightly grease 30 mini muffin holes. Sift the flour into a large bowl, add the polenta, baking powder, sugar and 1/2 teaspoon of salt and mix together well. Add the egg, butter and milk and stir until just combined. Spoon small amounts into the muffin holes, filling to the top. Cook for 15–20 minutes, or until lightly browned. Turn onto a cake rack to cool.

Mix together the dill, lemon juice, horseradish cream and mayonnaise, and season with plenty of salt and black pepper.

When the muffins are cool, cut a circle from the top, as you would with a butterfly cake, and spoon a little dill mayonnaise on the muffin. Top with a prawn and some freshly ground black pepper.

Makes 30

Slightly spicy and not too sweet, these babies are dangerously addictive little morsels and a sunny way to start the day.

baby banana breads with passionfruit butter

350 g (12 oz/1¹/₂ cups) caster (superfine) sugar
2 eggs
125 ml (4 fl oz/¹/₂ cup) vegetable oil
2 ripe bananas, mashed
215 g (7¹/₂ oz/1³/₄ cups) plain (all-purpose) flour
¹/₂ teaspoon baking powder
¹/₂ teaspoon ground cinnamon

passionfruit butter
250 g (9 oz/1 cup) spreadable cream cheese
3 tablespoons icing (confectioners') sugar
3 tablespoons passionfruit pulp, including the juice
2 teaspoons lemon juice

Preheat the oven to 180°C (350°F/Gas 4) and generously grease twelve 8 x 3 cm (3^1/4 x 1^1/4 inch) mini loaf tins.

In a large bowl, whisk together the sugar and eggs. Add the oil and 2 tablespoons of warm water. Whisk for 1 minute, then stir in the banana.

Sift the flour, baking powder and cinnamon into the bowl and stir to combine. Spoon the mixture into the tins and bake for 15–18 minutes, or until a skewer inserted into the centre comes out clean.

To make the passionfruit butter, combine the cream cheese and icing sugar in a food processor. Transfer to a bowl and stir in the passionfruit pulp. Add the lemon juice, a little at a time, to taste. Serve with the baby banana breads.

Makes 12

baby banana breads with passionfruit butter

chocolate strawberries

250 g (9 oz/1 punnet) large
    strawberries
150 g (5½ oz) good-quality
    dark chocolate

100 g (3½ oz) good-quality
    white chocolate

Remove the leaves from the strawberries and brush with a dry pastry brush to remove any dirt. Line a baking tray with baking paper.

Melt the dark chocolate in a small heatproof bowl over a saucepan of simmering water, making sure the bowl does not touch the water. Dip the bottom half of each strawberry in the chocolate, then transfer to the baking tray and leave to set.

When set, melt the white chocolate in a small heatproof bowl over a saucepan of simmering water, then dip the tips of the strawberries in the chocolate. Return to the baking tray and allow to set.

Makes about 12

fruit bites with warm chocolate sauce

fresh fruit, chopped into
  24 pieces
250 g (9 oz) good-quality
  dark chocolate

185 ml (6 fl oz/³/4 cup) cream
1 tablespoon golden syrup
2 tablespoons chocolate- or
  orange-flavoured liqueur

Thread three pieces of fruit onto eight small skewers.

Combine the chocolate, cream, golden syrup and liqueur in a small heatproof bowl. Put the bowl over a saucepan of simmering water, making sure the bowl does not touch the water, and stir until melted. Serve with the fruit skewers.

Makes 8

custard and fruit tarts

4 sheets ready-rolled sweet
    shortcrust pastry
1 vanilla pod
315 ml (11 fl oz/1¼ cups)
    milk
2 egg yolks
2 tablespoons sugar

3 tablespoons plain (all-purpose)
    flour
375 g (13 oz) mixed fruit (such
    as strawberries, blueberries,
    kiwifruit), cut into pieces
3 tablespoons apricot jam,
    warmed and sieved

Preheat the oven to 180°C (350°F/ Gas 4). Lightly grease 24 baby tart tins. Cut the pastry into 24 rectangles to fit the tart tins. Put the pastry in the tins and prick the bases several times with a fork. Bake for 12–15 minutes, or until golden brown. Remove and leave to cool.

Cut the vanilla pod in half and put in a saucepan with the milk. Slowly bring to the boil, then remove from the heat and cool slightly.

In a large heatproof bowl, whisk the egg yolks and sugar until thick and pale. Add the flour. Remove the vanilla pod from the milk, then gradually whisk the milk into the egg mixture. Return to a clean pan over medium heat and stir constantly for 5–10 minutes, or until the custard boils and thickens. Allow to cool, then spoon evenly into each pastry case and top with the fruit slices. Glaze with the warm apricot jam.

Makes 24

petits pithiviers

almond filling
45 g (1¹/₂ oz) butter
40 g (1¹/₂ oz/¹/₃ cup) icing
   (confectioners') sugar
1 egg yolk
70 g (2¹/₂ oz/²/₃ cup) ground
   almonds

1 teaspoon finely grated orange
   zest
few drops of almond essence

3 sheets ready-rolled puff pastry
1 egg, lightly beaten

To make the almond filling, beat the butter and icing sugar with electric beaters until light and creamy. Add the egg yolk and beat well. Stir in the ground almonds, orange zest and almond essence.

Lightly grease two baking trays. Lay the puff pastry on a work surface and cut into 48 rounds with a 5 cm (2 inch) cutter. Divide the almond filling among half the rounds, using about 1¹/₂ teaspoons of filling for each, and leaving a 5 mm (¹/₄ inch) border. Brush the border with beaten egg. Put the remaining pastry rounds over the filling and press the edges firmly to seal. Transfer to the baking trays and refrigerate for about 30 minutes. Preheat the oven to 210°C (415°F/Gas 6–7).

With a blunt-edged knife, gently press up the pastry edges at intervals. Carefully score the pastry tops into wedges, then brush with beaten egg. Bake for 10 minutes, or until lightly golden.

Makes 24

custard and fruit tarts

hot lazy days Blue skies and bright sunshine almost demand that you pack the snacks and head on out. Whether it's a picnic or a barbecue, a blanket on the lawn or just a chair on the balcony, outdoor food calls for a relaxed and languid vibe with unfussy food and minimal work in the field. A hamper and a corkscrew are the essentials to soak up the flavours of summertime.

Nibbles have the wonderful quality of being incredibly adaptable. It's so easy to throw together a menu that will satisfy the most diverse range of palates. When planning an outdoor lunch think of the menu as being like a tasting plate or a degustation menu — instead of offering your guests one large option, you can tantalize them with a carefully thought-out range of complementary flavours. Portability is a major consideration when planning a successful picnic. Presentation is always a priority but here the key is getting the food from A to B intact and at the right temperature. This isn't too hard if you're staying close to home and kicking back in the garden, but a trip further afield requires a little forward planning and a few extra tricks. Styrofoam boxes are plain but they will keep the food warm or cold for a good few hours. Or you could try tracking down some Indian tiffin trays, an excellent way of transporting hot food that looks fab too. Hampers work like they're meant to and always look pretty. Think of the outdoors as another room and put a bit of effort into dressing it up. Rugs and cushions make for comfortable lounging. Pretty napkins, plates and glasses all add to the effect. And garden torches can be lit when the afternoon heads for evening. If you want to go all out, fabrics draped in a tree can achieve a lovely effect. Then all you need is a bat, a ball, some delicious wines and fruit juices and a bunch of friends for a gorgeous afternoon in the sun.

Satay sticks are fabulous for picnics, barbecues or any outdoor meal — pack the spicy sauce and cook the skewers on the spot.

satay chicken skewers

12 chicken tenderloins, trimmed
   and halved lengthways
1 garlic clove, crushed
3 teaspoons fish sauce
2 teaspoons grated fresh ginger
lime quarters, to serve

satay sauce
2 teaspoons peanut oil
4 red Asian shallots, finely chopped
2 garlic cloves, chopped
2 teaspoons grated fresh ginger
2 small red chillies, seeded and finely chopped
200 ml (7 fl oz) coconut milk
125 g (4^1/$_2$ oz/^{1}/$_2$ cup) crunchy peanut butter
2 tablespoons grated palm sugar or soft brown sugar

2 tablespoons lime juice
1¹/₂ tablespoons fish sauce
2 teaspoons soy sauce
1 makrut (kaffir lime) leaf

Soak 24 wooden skewers in water for 1 hour. Combine the chicken, garlic, fish sauce and ginger. Cover, then refrigerate for 1 hour.

To make the satay sauce, heat the oil in a saucepan over medium heat. Add the shallots, garlic, ginger and chilli and cook for 5 minutes, or until golden. Add the rest of the ingredients, then reduce the heat and simmer for 10 minutes, or until thick.

Thread each chicken strip onto a skewer, then cook on a hot barbecue hotplate or chargrill pan (griddle) for 3–4 minutes, turning during cooking. Serve with satay sauce and lime wedges.

Makes 24

satay chicken skewers

garlic lamb skewers

600 g (1 lb 5 oz) trimmed
    lamb steaks, cut into 2 cm
    (³/4 inch) cubes
6 garlic cloves, cut into thick
    slices

marinade
1 red chilli, seeded and chopped
2 garlic cloves, crushed
3 tablespoons oil, plus extra
    for brushing

Thread two lamb cubes and two slices of garlic alternately onto 24 small metal skewers.

To make the marinade, mix together the chilli, garlic and oil.

Heat a barbecue hot plate or chargrill pan (griddle) over high heat and lightly brush with oil. Cook the skewers for 4–5 minutes, turning and brushing occasionally with the marinade.

Makes 24

chilli vegetables

12 baby corn cobs, halved
12 shiitake mushrooms, halved
12 snowpeas (mangetout),
    halved

2 tablespoons oil, plus extra
    for brushing
1 garlic clove, crushed
1 tablespoon sweet chilli sauce

Soak 24 small wooden skewers in water for 1 hour. Thread the corn, mushrooms and snowpeas alternately onto the skewers.

Mix together the oil, garlic and sweet chilli sauce in a bowl and brush over the skewers.

Heat a barbecue hot plate or chargrill pan (griddle) over high heat and lightly brush with oil. Cook the skewers for 3–4 minutes, turning and brushing with the chilli oil during cooking.

Makes 24

dolmades

200 g (7 oz) packet vine leaves in brine
250 g (9 oz/1 cup) medium-grain rice
1 small onion, finely chopped
1 tablespoon olive oil
50 g (1³/4 oz/¹/3 cup) pine nuts, toasted
2 tablespoons currants
2 tablespoons chopped dill
2 tablespoons finely chopped mint
2 tablespoons finely chopped flat-leaf (Italian) parsley
4 tablespoons olive oil, extra
2 tablespoons lemon juice
500 ml (17 fl oz/2 cups) chicken or vegetable stock

Put the vine leaves in a bowl, cover with cold water and soak for about 15 minutes. Remove, pat dry and cut off any stems. Reserve five or six leaves; discard any with holes. Meanwhile, pour boiling water over the rice and soak for 10 minutes, then drain.

Put the rice, onion, olive oil, pine nuts, currants and herbs in a large bowl. Season with salt and pepper and mix well.

Lay some leaves vein-side-down on a flat surface. Put $^1/_2$ tablespoon of filling in the middle of each leaf, fold the stalk end over the filling, then the left and right sides into the middle, and finally roll firmly towards the tip. The dolmade should resemble a small fat cigar. Repeat with the remaining filling and leaves to make 48 dolmades.

Line the base of a large heavy-based saucepan or flameproof casserole with the reserved leaves. Drizzle with 1 tablespoon of the extra oil. Put the dolmades in the pan, tightly packing them in one layer. Pour the lemon juice and remaining oil over them.

Pour the stock over the dolmades and cover with an inverted plate to stop them moving while cooking. Bring to the boil, then reduce the heat and simmer gently, covered, for 45 minutes. Remove with a slotted spoon. Serve warm or cold.

Makes 48

garlic lamb skewers and dolmades

tzatziki

1 Lebanese (short) cucumber
2 garlic cloves, crushed
250 g (9 oz/1 cup) plain yoghurt
1 teaspoon white vinegar
1 teaspoon chopped dill
1 teaspoon chopped mint

Finely grate the cucumber and squeeze out the excess moisture. Transfer to a bowl with the garlic, yoghurt, vinegar, dill and mint, season to taste with salt and freshly ground black pepper and mix together well. Serve with spring onion flatbreads (see page 56).

Serves 6–8

taramasalata

4 slices white bread, crusts
    removed
4 tablespoons milk
200 g (7 oz) smoked cod or
    grey mullet roe
1 egg yolk

1 garlic clove, crushed
150–170 ml (5–5$\frac{1}{2}$ fl oz)
    olive oil
2 tablespoons lemon juice
1 tablespoon finely chopped
    parsley

Soak the bread in the milk for 5 minutes. Squeeze out the excess liquid and transfer to a food processor.

Add the roe, egg yolk and garlic and process until smooth. With the motor running, slowly pour in the oil, stopping when the mixture is thick and holds its form. Stir in the lemon juice and parsley. Season and add more lemon juice, if needed. If you prefer a deeper colour, you can add a few drops of red food colouring. Serve with spring onion flatbreads (see page 56).

Serves 6–8

Bursting with the sweet heat of spring onions, these little flatbreads are easy to make and utterly delicious for dipping.

spring onion flatbreads

2 teaspoons oil
170 g (6 oz/1 bunch) spring onions (scallions), thinly sliced
1 garlic clove, crushed
215 g (7^1/$_2$ oz/1^3/$_4$ cups) plain (all-purpose) flour
1^1/$_2$ tablespoons chopped coriander (cilantro) leaves
oil, for pan-frying

Heat the oil in a frying pan, add the spring onion and garlic and cook for 2–3 minutes, or until soft.

Combine the flour and 1 teaspoon of salt in a large bowl. Add the onion mixture and chopped coriander. Gradually stir in 250 ml (9 fl oz/1 cup) of boiling water, stopping when a loose dough forms. Knead the dough with floured hands for 1^1/$_2$–2 minutes, or until smooth. Cover with plastic wrap and rest for 30 minutes.

Break off walnut-sized pieces of dough and roll out into 20 thin ovals. Fill a large frying pan with 2 cm (^{3}/4 inch) of oil and heat over medium heat. When shimmering, cook the breads two or three at a time for about 25–30 seconds each side, or until crisp and golden. Drain on paper towels and serve warm.

Makes 20

spring onion flatbreads with taramasalata and tzatziki

creamy herb mini quiches

2 sheets ready-rolled shortcrust
   pastry
2 eggs, beaten
2 tablespoons milk
125 ml (4 fl oz/1/2 cup) cream
2 teaspoons chopped chives

1 teaspoon chopped dill
1 teaspoon chopped thyme
1 teaspoon chopped parsley
2 tablespoons grated Parmesan
   cheese

Preheat the oven to 200°C (400°F/Gas 6). Lightly grease 24 mini tart tins. Lay the pastry sheets on a work surface and cut out 24 shapes to fit the tins. Line the tins with pastry.

Mix together the beaten egg, milk, cream, chives, dill, thyme and parsley. Pour into the pastry cases and sprinkle with the grated Parmesan. Bake for 15–20 minutes, or until puffed and golden. Remove from the tins while warm and cool on wire racks.

Makes 24

smoked salmon mini quiches

2 sheets ready-rolled shortcrust
pastry
100 g (3¹/₂ oz) cream cheese
3 tablespoons cream
2 eggs

100 g (3¹/₂ oz) smoked salmon,
finely chopped
3 tablespoons salmon roe
small dill sprigs, to garnish

Preheat the oven to 200°C (400°F/Gas 6). Lightly grease 24 mini tart tins. Lay the pastry sheets on a work surface and cut out 24 shapes to fit the tins. Line the tins with pastry.

Put the cream cheese, cream and eggs in a food processor and mix together, then add some cracked black pepper, to taste. Sprinkle a little smoked salmon into each pastry case, then pour the cream cheese mixture over the top. Bake for 15–20 minutes, or until puffed and golden. Remove from the tins while warm and cool on wire racks. Top with a little salmon roe and a sprig of dill before serving.

Makes 24

smoked salmon mini quiches

These crunchy little chicken strips mix the bite of nutty macadamias with the spicy sweetness of mango salsa.

macadamia-crusted chicken strips with mango salsa

12 chicken tenderloins
seasoned plain (all-purpose) flour, for coating
2 eggs, lightly beaten
240 g (8^3/$_4$ oz/1^1/$_2$ cups) macadamias,
    finely chopped
160 g (5^3/$_4$ oz/2 cups) fresh breadcrumbs
oil, for deep-frying

mango salsa
1 small mango, very finely diced
2 tablespoons finely diced red onion
2 tablespoons roughly chopped coriander
    (cilantro) leaves
1 green chilli, seeded and finely chopped
1 tablespoon lime juice

Cut the chicken into strips and dust with the flour. Dip the strips in the egg, then coat them in the combined nuts and breadcrumbs. Refrigerate for at least 30 minutes to firm up.

To make the salsa, combine all the ingredients in a small bowl and season to taste with salt and pepper.

Fill a large heavy-based saucepan one-third full of oil and heat to 180°C (350°F), or until a cube of bread dropped in the oil browns in 15 seconds. Cook the chicken strips in batches for 2–3 minutes, or until golden brown all over, taking care not to burn the nuts. Drain well on crumpled paper towels. Serve warm with the salsa.

Makes about 24

macadamia-crusted chicken strips with mango salsa

classic brownies

125 g (4 1/2 oz/1 cup) plain
  (all-purpose) flour
1/2 teaspoon baking powder
150 g (5 1/2 oz) good-quality
  dark chocolate
90 g (3 1/4 oz) unsalted butter

2 eggs, lightly beaten
170 g (6 oz/3/4 cup) caster
  (superfine) sugar
1 teaspoon vanilla essence
100 g (3 1/2 oz) milk chocolate
  bits (chips)

Preheat the oven to 180°C (350°F/Gas 4). Lightly grease a shallow 20 cm (8 inch) square cake tin and line the base and sides with baking paper, leaving the paper hanging over two opposite sides.

Sift the flour and baking powder together. Chop the chocolate and butter into small even-sized pieces and put in a heatproof bowl. Bring a saucepan of water to the boil, then remove from the heat. Sit the bowl over the saucepan, making sure the bowl does not touch the water. Leave, stirring occasionally, until the chocolate and butter have melted. Cool slightly.

Put the eggs, sugar and vanilla essence in a bowl and beat with electric beaters for 2 minutes, or until pale and thick. Stir in the melted chocolate mixture. Fold in the flour with a metal spoon until combined, then add the chocolate bits and mix well. Spoon into the tin and bake for 30 minutes, or until a skewer inserted in the centre comes out clean. Leave in the tin for 10 minutes, then cool completely on a wire rack. Cut into squares.

Makes 16 pieces

pecan brownies

125 g (4¹/₂ oz) good-quality
    dark chocolate
90 g (3¹/₄ oz) unsalted butter,
    softened
230 g (8 oz/1 cup) caster
    (superfine) sugar
1 teaspoon vanilla essence

2 eggs
85 g (3 oz/²/₃ cup) plain
    (all-purpose) flour
30 g (1 oz/¹/₄ cup) cocoa powder
¹/₂ teaspoon baking powder
125 g (4¹/₂ oz/1 cup) roughly
    chopped pecans

Preheat the oven to 180°C (350°F/Gas 4). Lightly grease a shallow 17 cm (6¹/₂ inch) square cake tin and line the base and sides with baking paper, leaving the paper hanging over two opposite sides.

Chop the chocolate into small even-sized pieces and put in a heatproof bowl. Bring a saucepan of water to the boil, then remove from the heat. Sit the bowl over the saucepan, making sure the bowl does not touch the water. Leave, stirring occasionally, until melted. Cool slightly.

Beat the butter, sugar and vanilla with electric beaters until thick and creamy. Add the eggs one at a time, beating well after each addition. Stir in the chocolate. Sift the flour, cocoa and baking powder and fold in with a metal spoon, then fold in the pecans. Spoon into the tin and smooth the surface. Bake for 30–35 minutes, or until firm and it comes away from the sides of the tin. Cool in the tin, remove and cut into squares.

Makes 16 pieces

passionfruit and coconut cheese slice

100 g (3^1/$_2$ oz/^{2}/$_3$ cup) blanched almonds
125 g (4^1/$_2$ oz/1 cup) plain (all-purpose) flour
1 teaspoon baking powder
100 g (3^1/$_2$ oz) unsalted butter, chopped
115 g (4 oz/^{1}/$_2$ cup) caster (superfine) sugar
2 eggs, plus 1 egg yolk
25 g (1 oz/^{1}/$_4$ cup) desiccated coconut
600 g (1 lb 5 oz/2^1/$_3$ cups) cream cheese
125 ml (4 fl oz/^{1}/$_2$ cup) coconut milk
3 teaspoons vanilla essence
^{1}/$_2$ teaspoon lemon juice
170 g (6 oz/^{3}/$_4$ cup) caster (superfine) sugar, extra
90 g (3^1/$_4$ oz/^{3}/$_4$ cup) icing (confectioners') sugar
40 g (1^1/$_2$ oz) unsalted butter, extra, softened
1 tablespoon cornflour (cornstarch)
2 tablespoons strained passionfruit juice
40 g (1^1/$_2$ oz/^{3}/$_4$ cup) flaked coconut

Finely chop the almonds in a food processor. Sift the flour and baking powder into a large bowl. Add the butter and rub into the flour with your fingertips until it resembles breadcrumbs. Stir in the almonds and sugar.

Make a well in the centre and add the egg yolk. Mix with a flat-bladed knife, using a cutting action, until the mixture comes together in beads. Add 2 tablespoons of cold water if needed. Gently gather the mixture together and put on a lightly floured work surface. Shape into a ball, flatten slightly, then wrap in plastic wrap and refrigerate for 30 minutes.

Preheat the oven to 170°C (325°F/Gas 3). Lightly grease a 27 x 18 x 5 cm (10³/₄ x 7 x 2 inch) tin and line with baking paper, hanging over the two long sides. Roll out the dough to fit the base of the tin and press in evenly. Sprinkle the coconut over the base and lightly press it in. Bake for about 10 minutes, then cool for 10 minutes.

Combine the cream cheese and whole eggs in a food processor. Add the coconut milk, vanilla, lemon juice and extra sugar and blend until smooth. Pour over the base and bake for 40 minutes, or until firm. Cool in the tin.

Mix the icing sugar and extra butter with a wooden spoon until smooth. Stir in the cornflour, then gradually add the passionfruit juice. Mix until smooth. Using a 5 cm (2 inch) cutter, cut out 12 rounds from the cooled cake. Spread the icing on thickly and top with the flaked coconut.

Makes 12 pieces

passionfruit and coconut cheese slice

teatime A delicious combination of elegance and sophistication, tea is back on the menu after years in the wilderness. Sandwiches and scones, chocolates and cakes, scaled down and layered up,

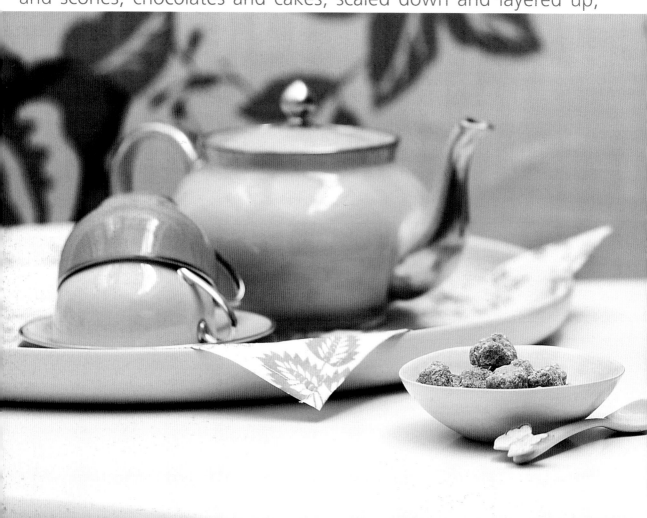

provide for indulgent grazing. Tea and loads of Champagne are all you need to complete the menu for your baby shower, hen's night or any other occasion that calls for a gathering of the girls.

There is a defined order and spread of delights associated with the classic afternoon tea that provides a wonderful framework within which to plan the menu. There should be a range of savouries, cakes, biscuits and scones to achieve the full effect of a sumptuous tea. Traditional menus served up an array of sandwiches, usually cucumber, roast beef and smoked salmon, then a selection of miniature cakes, biscuits and scones with jam and cream. From this basis you can add a deliciously wide range of recipes — feel free to serve whatever you wish, but the rule is to keep it small and delicate. Serving it up is half the fun, and a tea for the girls is the ideal time to indulge your feminine side. Flowers, napkins, crystal and silver all set the tone for an afternoon of quiet luxury. A mismatched set of fine china teacups in old-fashioned floral prints makes for an unconventional yet elegant look. For those of you with a secret penchant for doilies, there is no better time to indulge. Tea, coffee, hot chocolate and perhaps Champagne are all you need to complete the meal. Offer a range of loose teas and make sure you have a couple of teapots to hand; this is not the time for a tea bag in a chipped mug, it's more about putting on the Ritz at home. Elegant dainties, fortifying brews and conversation are the key pleasures of a classic afternoon tea.

marinated trout and cucumber tarts

filling
300 g (10¹/₂ oz) ocean trout fillet
3 tablespoons lemon juice
2 tablespoons extra virgin olive oil
¹/₂ small Lebanese (short) cucumber, finely chopped
2 spring onions (scallions), finely sliced
24 baby English spinach leaves
24 dill sprigs

125 g (4¹/₂ oz/1 cup) plain (all-purpose) flour
2 tablespoons grated Parmesan cheese
75 g (2¹/₂ oz) chilled butter, cubed
1 egg, lightly beaten

To make the filling, remove the skin from the trout, then, using kitchen tweezers, take out the bones. Freeze the fish in plastic wrap for about 1 hour. Whisk the lemon juice and oil in a bowl. Cut the fish into 3 x 1 cm (1¹/₄ x ¹/₂ inch) strips and add to the lemon marinade. Leave, covered, at room temperature for 20 minutes, or until the fish turns opaque (in summer, refrigerate — this will take a little longer). Drain off most of the marinade, leaving just enough to moisten the fish. Add the cucumber and spring onion. Season.

Sift the flour and a pinch of salt into a large bowl and add the Parmesan and butter. Rub in with your fingertips until the mixture resembles fine breadcrumbs. Make a well. Stir in the egg with a flat-bladed knife until the mixture comes together in beads. Turn onto a lightly floured surface and gather into a ball. Wrap in plastic wrap and refrigerate for 30 minutes.

Preheat the oven to 200°C (400°F/Gas 6). Lightly grease 24 round-based tart tins. Roll out the pastry to about 2 mm (^{1}/16 inch) thick and cut out 24 x 6 cm (2^1/2 inch) rounds (the pastry cases will be smaller than the tins). Prick the pastry lightly with a fork and bake for 8 minutes, or until golden. Remove from the tins and set aside to cool. Put a spinach leaf in each tart case and spoon on 1 level tablespoon of filling. Top with a dill sprig.

Makes 24

marinated trout and cucumber tarts

mini focaccia with roasted vegetables

2 red capsicums (peppers), cut into 3 cm (1¼ inch) pieces

2 yellow capsicums (peppers), cut into 3 cm (1¼ inch) pieces

3 slender eggplants (aubergines), cut into 1 cm (½ inch) rounds

2 large zucchini (courgettes), cut into 1 cm (½ inch) rounds

1 red onion, thinly sliced

4 tablespoons extra virgin olive oil

3 garlic cloves, crushed

12 mini focaccias, split in half

3 tablespoons ready-made or home-made pesto

3 large fresh bocconcini cheese, sliced

Preheat the oven to 200°C (400°F/Gas 6). Put all the vegetables in a large roasting tin with the oil and garlic, season with salt and cracked black pepper and toss together well. Roast for 25 minutes, or until cooked.

Spread each focaccia half with ½ teaspoon of pesto. Arrange the roasted vegetables over each base, top with two slices of bocconcini, then sandwich with the lids. Toast on both sides on a hot chargrill pan (griddle).

Cut each focaccia in half (or quarters, depending on the size of the focaccia), then wrap a wide band of paper around the middle of the sandwiches. Serve warm.

Makes 24

sweet potato rosti

3 orange sweet potatoes,
   unpeeled
2 teaspoons cornflour
   (cornstarch)

40 g (1^1/$_2$ oz) butter
150 g (5^1/$_2$ oz) mozzarella cheese,
   cut into 30 cubes

Boil the sweet potatoes until almost cooked, but still firm. Set aside to cool, then peel and coarsely grate into a bowl. Add the cornflour and ^{1}/$_2$ teaspoon of salt and toss lightly to combine.

Melt a little of the butter in a frying pan over low heat. Put teaspoons of the potato mixture in the pan and press a cube of cheese in the centre of each mound. Top with another teaspoon of potato and gently flatten to form rough circles. Increase the heat to medium and cook for 3 minutes on each side, or until golden. Remove and drain on paper towels. Repeat with remaining potato mixture and mozzarella cubes. Serve hot.

Makes 30

Sharp, pungent Stilton lends a serious bite to these delectable scones, yet is softened by the deep sweetness of the syrupy figs.

mini scones with ham and port figs

scones
2 cups (250 g/9 oz) plain
   (all-purpose) flour
3 teaspoons baking powder
110 g (3³/4 oz) chilled butter
100 g (3¹/2 oz) Stilton cheese
2 tablespoons chopped chives
185 ml (6 fl oz/³/4 cup) milk

250 ml (9 fl oz/1 cup) port
6 large dried figs, stems
   removed
1 teaspoon sugar
2 teaspoons Dijon mustard
4 tablespoons sour cream
150 g (5¹/2 oz) shaved ham
garlic chives, to garnish

To make the scones, sift the flour, baking powder and ³/4 teaspoon of salt into a large bowl. Coarsely grate the butter and cheese into the flour and rub in with your fingertips until the mixture resembles coarse breadcrumbs. Stir in the chives. Pour in the milk and mix with a flat-bladed knife until the mixture comes together in beads. Turn onto a floured surface and press into a ball.

On a floured surface, roll the dough into a 15 x 25 cm (6 x 10 inch) rectangle. With the long edge of the dough facing you, fold in both ends so they meet in the centre, then fold the dough in half widthways. Roll again into a 15 x 25 cm (6 x 10 inch) rectangle, about 1 cm ($^1/_2$ inch) thick. Cut rounds close together with a 4 cm ($1^1/_2$ inch) cutter. Push the scraps together and roll and cut as before. Arrange the scones 2.5 cm (1 inch) apart on a baking tray and refrigerate for 20 minutes. Preheat the oven to 220°C (425°F/Gas 7). Bake for 10–12 minutes, or until lightly browned.

Heat the port, figs and sugar in a small saucepan. Bring to the boil, then reduce the heat and simmer for 15 minutes. Remove the figs. Simmer the liquid for 3 minutes, until reduced and syrupy. Cut each fig into 3 pieces.

Cut the top off the scones and discard. Combine the mustard and sour cream and spread over the scone bottoms. Top with a folded piece of ham. Put a piece of fig on top and drizzle with fig syrup. Top with garlic chives.

Makes 18

mini focaccia with roasted vegetables

mini scones with ham and port figs

chicken and guacamole squares

guacamole
2 avocados
1 tablespoon mayonnaise
1 teaspoon chopped seeded
    chilli
1 tablespoon lemon juice
1 small tomato, chopped
1/2 red onion, finely chopped

8 slices wholemeal bread,
    crusts removed
250 g (9 oz) sliced smoked
    chicken breast
30 g (1 oz/1 cup) snowpea
    (mangetout) sprouts,
    trimmed
25 g (1 oz) butter

To make the guacamole, mash the avocados with the mayonnaise, chilli, lemon juice, tomato and onion.

Spread the guacamole over four slices of bread and top with the chicken slices. Add the snowpea sprouts. Butter the remaining bread slices and press onto the sprouts. Cut each sandwich into four squares and serve.

Makes 16

turkey and brie triangles

8 slices bread, crusts removed
1½ tablespoons cranberry sauce
125 g (4½ oz) sliced turkey
    breast

125 g (4½ oz) Brie cheese,
    sliced
4 butter lettuce leaves

Spread four slices of bread with cranberry sauce. Arrange the turkey breast, Brie and lettuce leaves over the sauce, then sandwich with the remaining bread slices. Cut each sandwich into four triangles and serve.

Makes 16

herbed pikelets with pear and blue cheese topping

125 g (4$^{1}/_{2}$ oz/1 cup) self-raising flour
2 eggs, lightly beaten
125 ml (4 fl oz/$^{1}/_{2}$ cup) milk
2 tablespoons finely chopped parsley
2 teaspoons finely chopped sage
cooking oil spray, for pan-frying

pear and blue cheese topping
100 g (3$^{1}/_{2}$ oz) Blue Castello or other creamy blue cheese
75 g (2$^{1}/_{2}$ oz) cream cheese
2 teaspoons brandy
1 large, ripe green-skinned pear
30 g (1 oz/$^{1}/_{4}$ cup) finely chopped toasted walnuts
$^{1}/_{2}$ lemon
1$^{1}/_{2}$ tablespoons finely chopped chives

Sift the flour into a bowl and make a well in the centre. Gradually add the combined eggs and milk, mixing the flour in slowly. When the flour is incorporated, add the parsley and sage and season well with salt and cracked black pepper. Whisk until a smooth batter forms.

Heat a large non-stick frying pan over medium heat and spray with cooking oil spray. Drop heaped teaspoons of batter into the pan and flatten them a little to give 5 cm (2 inch) rounds. Cook until bubbles appear on the surface of the pikelets, then turn and brown the other side. Lift onto a wire rack to cool.

To make the topping, beat the cheeses and brandy together until smooth. Season with pepper. Cut the pear in half. Peel and core one half of it, then cut it into 5 mm (1/4 inch) dice, leaving the rest of the pear untouched. Stir the diced pear into the cheese mixture along with the walnuts.

Core the other half of the pear but do not peel it. Cut it into thin slices along its length (so that each slice has one border with the skin on). Cut these into 2 cm (3/4 inch) triangles with one slightly curved side having green skin. Squeeze some lemon juice over the cut surfaces to prevent discolouration.

Pile 1 teaspoon of topping in the centre of each pikelet and flatten it slightly to cover most of the surface. Arrange two of the pear triangles on top in a row, overlapping one another. Sprinkle with chives.

Makes 36

herbed pikelets with pear and blue cheese topping

mini lime meringue pies

4 sheets ready-rolled sweet
    shortcrust pastry
115 g (4 oz/$1/2$ cup) caster
    (superfine) sugar
30 g (1 oz/$1/4$ cup) cornflour
    (cornstarch)
2 teaspoons grated lime zest

4 tablespoons lime juice
30 g (1 oz) butter
2 egg yolks
3 egg whites
115 g (4 oz/$1/2$ cup) caster
    (superfine) sugar, extra

Preheat the oven to 180°C (350°F/Gas 4). Grease two shallow 12-hole patty tins. Using a 7 cm ($2^3/4$ inch) cutter, cut 24 rounds from the pastry sheets. Put the rounds in the tins and prick the bases well with a fork. Bake for 12–15 minutes, or until golden brown, then cool.

Put the sugar, cornflour, lime zest, lime juice and 185 ml (6 fl oz/$3/4$ cup) of water in a large saucepan. Stir over medium heat until the mixture boils and thickens. Remove from the heat and add the butter. Mix well, then gradually stir in the egg yolks. Spoon 1 heaped teaspoon of the mixture into each pastry case.

Beat the egg whites with electric beaters until stiff peaks form. Gradually add the extra sugar and beat until it dissolves and the mixture is glossy. Spoon 1 tablespoon over each pie. Bake for 4–5 minutes, or until golden.

Makes 24

amaretti

1 tablespoon plain (all-purpose) flour
1 tablespoon cornflour (cornstarch)
1 teaspoon ground cinnamon
145 g (5¼ oz/⅔ cup) caster (superfine) sugar
1 teaspoon grated lemon zest
185 g (6½ oz/1 cup) ground almonds
2 egg whites
30 g (1 oz/¼ cup) icing (confectioners') sugar
candied lemon zest, to serve

Line two baking trays with baking paper. Sift the flours, cinnamon and half the caster sugar into a large bowl. Add the lemon zest and almonds.

Put the egg whites in a small, dry bowl. Beat with electric beaters until soft peaks form. Add the remaining caster sugar gradually, beating constantly until the mixture is thick and glossy and all the sugar has dissolved. Fold into the dry ingredients using a metal spoon. Stir until the mixture is just combined and forms a soft dough. With oiled or wet hands, roll 2 level teaspoons of mixture at a time into a ball. Arrange on the baking trays, allowing room for spreading. Set aside, uncovered, for 1 hour.

Preheat the oven to 180°C (350°F/Gas 4). Sift the icing sugar liberally over the biscuits. Bake for 15–20 minutes, or until crisp and lightly browned. Transfer to a wire rack to cool. Top with candied lemon zest and serve.

Makes 24

mini lime meringue pies

amaretti

baby florentines

90 g (3¼ oz) butter
115 g (4 oz/½ cup) caster
    (superfine) sugar
1 tablespoon honey
45 g (1½ oz/heaped ⅓ cup)
    slivered almonds, chopped
45 g (1¾ oz) mixed peel

60 g (2¼ oz/⅓ cup) dried
    apricots, finely chopped
2 tablespoons chopped glacé
    cherries
60 g (2¼ oz/½ cup) plain
    (all-purpose) flour
150 g (5½ oz) dark chocolate

Preheat the oven to 180°C (350°F/Gas 4). Cover two baking trays with baking paper. Melt the butter, sugar and honey in a saucepan. Remove from the heat and stir in the almonds, fruit and the flour. Roll teaspoons of the mixture into balls and arrange on the trays, allowing room for spreading. Press lightly with your fingertips into 3 cm (1¼ inch) rounds.

Bake for 8–10 minutes, or until golden. Cool on the trays until slightly firm. Using a spatula, carefully remove and cool completely on wire racks.

Bring a saucepan of water to the boil and remove from the heat. Put the chocolate in a heatproof bowl and sit the bowl over the pan, making sure the bowl does not touch the water. Stir occasionally until the chocolate has melted. Spread a thin layer of chocolate quickly over the backs of the florentines, then leave to set, chocolate-side-up.

Makes about 50

orange and almond friands

165 g (5³/4 oz/1¹/3 cups) icing
(confectioners') sugar
50 g (1³/4 oz/heaped ¹/3 cup)
plain (all-purpose) flour
100 g (3¹/2 oz/1 cup) ground
almonds
3 egg whites
150 g (5¹/2 oz) butter, melted
and strained

2 teaspoons orange zest
¹/4 teaspoon orange flower
water
icing (confectioners') sugar,
extra, for dusting
Persian fairy floss and orange
zest, to garnish (optional)

Preheat the oven to 180°C (350°F/Gas 4). Grease 30 x 20 ml (¹/2 fl oz) mini cake tins. Sift the icing sugar and flour into a bowl, add the ground almonds and mix well.

Beat the egg whites until soft peaks form and fold into the mixture. Add the butter, orange zest and orange flower water and stir well.

Spoon the mixture into the tins and bake for 8 minutes. Remove and cool slightly before removing from the tray and dusting with icing sugar. Garnish with a swirl of Persian fairy floss (available from Middle Eastern food stores) and some orange zest.

Makes 30

high heels and cocktails Hit the cocktail hour and the party really starts. When the dresses are slinkier and the liquor harder, the food needs to edge up a notch or more. Forget about keeping it simple, this is your chance to go all out and show what you can do. Be creative, be adventurous because there's no such thing as over the top when it comes to the true home of the canapé.

Weddings, **birthdays**, anniversaries — any event that demands proper celebration is the perfect excuse, should you need one, to throw a cocktail party. As the name suggests, at a cocktail **party** the food and drinks are of equal importance and it's the equal part that's paramount. The biggest, and most common, mistake made at cocktail parties is when the **drinks** are prioritized at the expense of the food. Unless you want things to get really messy it's wise to make sure there is plenty of food to go around. If your guests have to **pounce** on the trays, the food isn't coming out quick enough and if the room starts **spinning**, it's not substantial enough. Make sure there's a good mix of light food and some dishes with substance. It's also important to cater to all tastes and preferences with an **inventive** mix of spicy and non-spicy, seafood, meat and vegetarian. Of all possible events, cocktail parties require the most planning, the largest investment and the biggest army of helpers, but the result, when you pull it off, is its own reward. Recruit some friends to help decorate, prepare, cook and serve so you have time to **mingle**. You might like to delegate the creation of cocktails to a couple of experienced mixologists, amateur or otherwise. Leave yourself a little bit of time to change and freshen up, then take a deep breath, get the ball rolling and enjoy a **sparkling** evening.

Delicate and delicious, these rolls are perfect for the cocktail hour, offering a flawless mouthful without being a handful.

vietnamese rice paper rolls

nuoc cham dipping sauce
185 ml (6 fl oz/$3/4$ cup) fish sauce
3 tablespoons lime juice
2 tablespoons grated palm sugar or soft brown sugar
2 bird's eye chillies, seeded and finely chopped

150 g (5$1/2$ oz) dried rice vermicelli
48 x 15 cm (6 inch) round rice paper wrappers
48 cooked king prawns (shrimp), peeled, deveined
    and halved lengthways
150 g (5$1/2$ oz/1$2/3$ cups) bean sprouts
3 large handfuls Vietnamese mint
2 large handfuls coriander (cilantro) leaves
2 Lebanese (short) cucumbers, cut in half lengthways,
    seeded and cut into thin strips

To make the dipping sauce, combine all the ingredients and 125 ml (4 fl oz/^{1}/$_2$ cup) of water and stir until the sugar has dissolved. Transfer to a small serving dish and set aside.

Put the noodles in a heatproof bowl, cover with boiling water and soak for 10 minutes. Drain.

Assemble the rolls one at a time. Dip a rice paper wrapper in a bowl of warm water for 30 seconds, or until it softens. Lay the wrapper on a work surface and put two prawn halves on the bottom third of the wrapper. Top with a few noodles, bean sprouts, three mint leaves, six coriander leaves and a cucumber strip, in that order. Ensure that the filling is neat and compact, then turn up the bottom of the wrapper to cover the filling. Holding the filling in place, fold in the two sides, then roll up.

Arrange on a platter, folded-side-down. Cover with a damp tea towel or plastic wrap until ready to serve. Serve with the dipping sauce.

Makes 48

vietnamese rice paper rolls

asian crab tarts

3 tablespoons lime juice
1 tablespoon fish sauce
1 tablespoon grated palm sugar
  or soft brown sugar
300 g (10¹/₂ oz) fresh crab meat,
  shredded and well drained
2 tablespoons chopped
  coriander (cilantro) leaves
1 tablespoon chopped
  Vietnamese mint

1 small red chilli, seeded
  and finely chopped
2 makrut (kaffir lime) leaves,
  finely shredded
24 pre-cooked cooked tartlet
  cases
24 small Vietnamese mint
  leaves

Combine the lime juice, fish sauce and sugar in a bowl and stir until the sugar has dissolved.

Add the crab meat, coriander, mint, chilli and shredded lime leaves and mix together well. Spoon the filling into the tartlet cases and garnish with the Vietnamese mint leaves.

Makes 24

wasabi crème fraîche oysters

24 fresh oysters on the half shell
80 ml (2¹/₂ fl oz/¹/₃ cup) crème
  fraîche
2 tablespoons whole-egg
  mayonnaise

1¹/₂ teaspoons wasabi paste
flying fish or fish roe, to garnish
small lime wedges, to garnish

Remove the oysters from their shells. Wash the shells with hot water
and pat dry. Replace the oysters and cover them with a damp cloth in
the refrigerator.

Put the crème fraîche, mayonnaise and wasabi paste in a bowl and whisk
until well combined.

Put a teaspoon of the mixture on top of each oyster, then garnish with the
roe and lime wedges.

Makes 24

asian crab tarts

Sesame oil in the pancake dough lends a subtle, nutty taste that brings out the flavour yet cuts through the richness of the duck.

peking duck rolls

125 g (4¹/₂ oz/1 cup) plain
    (all-purpose) flour
¹/₂ teaspoon sesame oil
¹/₂ large Chinese roast duck
6 spring onions (scallions), cut
    into 6 cm (2¹/₂ inch) lengths
    (24 pieces in total)

1 Lebanese (short) cucumber,
    seeded and cut into 6 cm x
    5 mm (2¹/₂ x ¹/₄ inch) batons
2–3 tablespoons hoisin sauce
2 teaspoons sesame seeds,
    toasted
24 chives, blanched

Sift the flour into a small bowl, make a well in the centre and pour in the sesame oil and 125 ml (4 fl oz/¹/₂ cup) of boiling water. Mix well until it forms a slightly sticky soft dough (add a few more teaspoons of boiling water if the mixture is still a bit dry). Knead the dough on a floured work surface for 5 minutes, or until smooth. Cover and rest for 10 minutes.

Shred the duck meat into pieces with your fingers and cut the skin into small strips.

Roll the dough into a sausage shape and divide into 24 pieces. On a lightly floured board, roll each piece to an 8–9 cm (3^{1}/$_{4}$–3^{1}/$_{2}$ inch) round with a rolling pin. Once they are rolled out, lay out the rounds in a single layer and cover with plastic wrap or a clean tea towel while you are making the others to prevent them from drying out.

Heat a non-stick frying pan over medium heat and dry-fry the pancakes in batches for about 20 seconds on each side. Do not overcook, or they will become too crispy for rolling. The pancakes should have slight brown speckles on them. Stack each pancake on a plate, and keep warm. If they cool down too much, wrap them in foil and reheat in a warm (170°C/325°F/Gas 3) oven or microwave for 20–30 seconds on high.

Arrange a piece of spring onion, cucumber, duck flesh and skin on each pancake. Drizzle with ^{1}/$_{2}$ teaspoon of hoisin sauce and sprinkle with sesame seeds. Roll up firmly and tie each pancake with a blanched chive.

Makes 24

peking duck rolls

Fish and chips with mushy peas is rarely seen as a delicacy, but this modern interpretation will make you seriously reconsider.

scallops on potato crisps with pea purée

20 g (3/4 oz) butter
3 French shallots, finely chopped
1 garlic clove, finely chopped
2 slices mild pancetta, finely chopped
155 g (5 1/2 oz/1 cup) frozen peas
3 tablespoons chicken stock or water
oil, for deep-frying
2–3 floury potatoes (such as russet, King Edward),
    peeled and very thinly sliced to get 24 slices
24 scallops
mint leaves, to garnish

Melt the butter in a saucepan over low heat. Cook the shallots, garlic and pancetta for 3 minutes, or until soft but not coloured. Add the peas and stock. Cook over high heat for 3 minutes, or until the liquid has evaporated. Cool a little, then purée in a food processor until smooth. Season.

Fill a deep heavy-based saucepan one-third full of oil and heat to 190°C (375°F), or until a cube of bread dropped in the oil browns in 10 seconds. Cook the potato slices in batches until crisp and golden. Drain on crumpled paper towels and sprinkle with salt.

Toss the scallops with 1 tablespoon of oil. Season lightly. Heat a chargrill pan (griddle) to hot, then sear the scallops in batches for 5 seconds each side, or until lightly browned on the outside but opaque in the middle. Cut each scallop in half.

Reheat the pea purée. Spread a little on the bottom half of each scallop, then replace the top. Dollop 1 teaspoon of purée on each potato crisp, then top with a filled scallop. Season with pepper and garnish with mint.

Makes 24

scallops on potato crisps with pea purée

baby caviar potatoes

30 baby new potatoes (choose
    very small potatoes of a
    similar size)
250 g (9 oz/1 cup) sour cream

2 tablespoons caviar
    (red or black, or both)

Preheat the oven to 200°C (400°F/Gas 6). Prick the potatoes with a fork
and put them on a baking tray. Bake for 40 minutes, or until tender. Cool
to room temperature.

Cut a large cross in the top of each potato and squeeze open. Top with a
small dollop of sour cream and a little caviar.

Makes 30

chicken and tarragon cream vol au vents

1 small chicken breast fillet
250 ml (9 fl oz/1 cup) pure
    (single) cream
1 tablespoon finely chopped
    tarragon

1 spring onion (scallion), finely
    chopped
12 mini vol au vent pastry shells

Put the chicken fillet in a small saucepan of salted boiling water. Cover, turn off the heat and poach the chicken for about 20 minutes. Remove and cool before cutting the chicken into very small cubes. Preheat the oven to 170°C (325°F/Gas 3).

Put the cream in a small saucepan and bring to boiling point. Reduce the heat and simmer for 5–10 minutes, or until the cream is very thick. Stir in the chicken, tarragon and spring onion. While still warm, spoon the filling into the pastry shells, piling the filling up. Bake for 8 minutes. Serve hot.

Makes 12

chicken and tarragon cream vol au vents

wrapped prawns with mango dip

24 snowpeas (mangetout)
24 medium cooked prawns
   (shrimp), peeled and
   deveined

mango dip
125 g (4^1/$_2$ fl oz/^{1}/$_2$ cup)
   mayonnaise
2 tablespoons mango chutney
1 teaspoon curry paste
1 tablespoon lime juice

Blanch the snowpeas in boiling water for 30 seconds, or until tender. Drain and cool. Wrap them around the cooked prawns, then secure each one with a toothpick.

To make the dip, mix together the mayonnaise, mango chutney, curry paste and lime juice. Serve with the prawns.

Makes 24

grilled figs in prosciutto

25 g (1 oz) unsalted butter
1 tablespoon orange juice
12 small fresh figs
12 sage leaves

6 slices of prosciutto, trimmed
and halved lengthways

Put the butter in a small heavy-based saucepan. Melt over low heat, then cook the butter for 8–10 minutes, or until the froth subsides and the milk solids appear as brown specks on the bottom of the saucepan. Strain the butter into a clean bowl by pouring it through a strainer lined with a clean tea towel or paper towel. Stir the orange juice into the strained butter.

Gently cut a cross in the crown of each fig, cutting two-thirds of the way through. Gently squeeze the base — the top will open like a flower. Sit a sage leaf in the opening of each fig, then wrap a piece of prosciutto around each one, with the ends tucked under the bottom of the fig. Arrange the figs, cut-side-up, on a baking tray and brush lightly with the butter mixture.

Move the grill tray to its lowest position, then heat the grill (broiler) to hot. Put the tray of figs on the grill tray and cook for 1–1^1/$_2$ minutes, or until the prosciutto is slightly crispy. Serve warm or at room temperature.

Makes 12

grilled figs in prosciutto

pumpkin and hazelnut pesto bites

750 g (1 lb 10 oz) butternut
    pumpkin (squash), cut
    into 2.5 cm (1 inch) cubes
1¹/₂ tablespoons olive oil

hazelnut pesto
35 g (1¹/₄ oz/¹/₄ cup) toasted
    hazelnuts
35 g (1¹/₄ oz/1 cup) rocket
    (arugula)
1 tablespoon grated Parmesan
    cheese
3¹/₂ tablespoons olive oil

Preheat the oven to 200°C (400°F/Gas 6) and line a baking tray with baking paper. Toss the pumpkin cubes with the oil and some salt and pepper until evenly coated. Spread out on the baking tray and bake for 35 minutes, or until cooked.

To make the hazelnut pesto, process the hazelnuts, rocket, Parmesan and oil until they form a paste. Season to taste with salt and black pepper.

Spoon a small amount of the hazelnut pesto onto each piece of pumpkin and sprinkle with black pepper if desired. Serve warm or cold.

Makes about 20

feta, rocket and mushroom bruschetta

1 loaf Italian (ciabatta) bread
1 large garlic clove, peeled
extra virgin olive oil, to drizzle

topping
1 tablespoon olive oil
60 g (2^1/$_4$ oz) butter
300 g (10^1/$_2$ oz) Swiss brown
    mushrooms, quartered

2 garlic cloves, crushed
2 tablespoons roughly torn basil
150 g (5^1/$_2$ oz) soft marinated
    feta cheese
50 g (1^3/$_4$ oz/1^1/$_4$ cups) baby
    rocket (arugula) leaves

Preheat the oven to 200°C (400°F/Gas 6). Slice the bread on the diagonal into 12 x 1 cm (^{1}/$_2$ inch) thick slices. Lay the bread slices out in a single layer on a baking tray and bake for 10–12 minutes, or until lightly golden. Remove from the oven. Cut the garlic clove in half and rub over one side of each slice of toast, then lightly drizzle with oil. Cut them in half.

To make the topping, heat the oil and butter in a frying pan over high heat. Cook the mushrooms for 3–4 minutes, then add the garlic and cook for 1 minute. Remove the pan from the heat, stir in the basil and season to taste. Spread the feta on the bruschetta, and add a few rocket leaves. Top with some fried mushrooms, and serve immediately.

Makes 24

pumpkin and hazelnut pesto bites

parmesan wafers

125 g (4 1/2 oz/1 1/4 cups)
grated good-quality
Parmesan cheese

1 tablespoon flour
2 tablespoons thyme

Preheat the oven to 220°C (425°F/Gas 7). Line two baking trays with baking paper and, using a 7 cm (2 3/4 inch) cutter as a guide, draw circles on the paper. Turn the paper upside down on the trays. Toss the cheese and flour together in a bowl, then sprinkle 2 teaspoons of the mixture over three or four circles on the paper, spreading the mixture to the edge of each round. Scatter a few thyme leaves over each round.

Bake in batches for 3 minutes, or until melted but not firm. Using a spatula, turn the rounds over and cook for 1 minute more, or until they are firm and light golden. Remove each round from the tray and drape over a rolling pin or bottle until cool. Repeat to make 30 wafers.

Makes 30

olive basil cheese spread

250 g (9 oz/1 cup) cream cheese,
    softened
200 g (7 oz/1¹/₃ cups) feta
    cheese, crumbled

1 large handful basil leaves
3 tablespoons olive oil
15 Kalamata olives, pitted and
    roughly chopped

Combine the cream cheese, feta, basil, 1 tablespoon of the olive oil and
¹/₄ teaspoon of cracked black pepper in a bowl and mix until smooth.

Fold in the olives and spoon into a serving bowl. Smooth the top with the
back of the spoon. Pour the remaining oil over the top and garnish with
a little more cracked pepper. Delicious served with warm bread.

Serves 6–8

hot corn cakes with avocado and prawns

avocado sauce
1 ripe avocado, roughly chopped
2 tablespoons lime juice
1 tinned chipotle pepper, in sauce
1 handful coriander (cilantro) leaves
1 garlic clove, chopped
1 teaspoon ground cumin
2 tablespoons sour cream

60 g (2^1/$_4$ oz/^{1}/$_2$ cup) plain (all-purpose) flour
50 g (1^3/$_4$ oz/^{1}/$_3$ cup) polenta
^{1}/$_2$ teaspoon baking powder
^{1}/$_4$ teaspoon bicarbonate of soda
1 teaspoon salt
^{1}/$_2$ teaspoon sugar
250 ml (9 fl oz/1 cup) buttermilk
20 g (^{3}/$_4$ oz) butter, melted
1 egg
110 g (3^3/$_4$ oz/^{3}/$_4$ cup) frozen corn kernels, thawed, chopped
1^1/$_2$ tinned chipotle peppers, chopped, and 2 teaspoons of sauce
32 cooked prawns (shrimp), peeled and deveined
^{1}/$_2$ lime, sliced very thinly, cut into 32 small wedges, to garnish

To make the avocado sauce, put the ingredients and $1/2$ teaspoon of salt in a food processor and purée until very smooth. Season.

Combine the dry ingredients in a large bowl and make a well in the centre. Whisk the buttermilk, butter and egg together in a jug, gradually add to the dry ingredients and whisk until thoroughly incorporated. Roughly chop the corn and chipotle peppers in a food processor, then stir into the batter. (The batter should have the consistency of pancake batter — add a tablespoon of water to thin if necessary.)

Heat a lightly oiled frying pan over medium heat. Spoon tablespoons of the batter into the pan in batches, forming 5 cm (2 inch) cakes. Cook for 1 minute on each side, or until golden brown. Remove from the pan and keep warm while cooking the rest of the corn cakes.

Dollop a heaped teaspoon of avocado sauce on the warm corn cakes. Put one prawn on top and garnish with a tiny wedge of lime.

Makes 32

hot corn cakes with
avocado and prawns

beef rolls

500 g (1 lb 2 oz) beef fillet,
  8 cm (3¹/4 inches) in diameter
3 tablespoons olive oil
1¹/2 tablespoons horseradish
  cream
1¹/2 tablespoons wholegrain
  mustard
1 zucchini (courgette), cut into
  thin strips

1 small carrot, cut into thin
  strips
1 small red capsicum (pepper),
  cut into thin strips
60 g (2¹/4 oz) snowpeas
  (mangetout), cut into
  thin strips

Preheat the oven to 200°C (400°F/Gas 6). Trim the beef of excess fat and sinew and brush with a little of the oil. Heat a heavy-based frying pan over high heat and quickly brown each side of the beef fillet. Transfer to a baking dish and bake for 20 minutes. Remove and set aside to cool.

Slice the cooled beef very thinly. Combine the horseradish cream and the mustard, then spread a little over each slice of beef.

Heat the remaining oil in a saucepan over high heat and quickly cook the zucchini, carrot, capsicum and snowpeas. Cool. Put a small bunch of the vegetable strips on the end of each beef slice and roll up. Serve.

Makes about 20

devils and angels on horseback

4–6 streaky bacon rashers,
   cut into thin strips
12 pitted prunes
12 oysters, fresh or bottled

2 tablespoons Worcestershire
   sauce
Tabasco sauce, to taste

Soak 24 toothpicks in cold water for 1 hour to prevent them burning.

To make the devils, wrap a piece of bacon around each prune and secure with a skewer.

To make the angels, remove the oysters from their shells, or drain from the bottling liquid. Sprinkle lightly with Worcestershire sauce and some black pepper. Wrap each oyster in bacon, securing with a toothpick.

Preheat a lightly greased grill (broiler) or barbecue flatplate. Cook the savouries, turning occasionally, until the bacon is crisp. Serve sprinkled with a dash of Tabasco sauce.

Makes 24

salt and pepper squid

1 kg (2 lb 4 oz) small squid
    tubes
250 ml (9 fl oz/1 cup) lemon
    juice
250 g (9 oz/2 cups) cornflour
    (cornstarch)
2 tablespoons salt

1¹/₂ tablespoons ground white
    pepper
2 teaspoons caster (superfine)
    sugar
oil, for deep-frying
4 egg whites, lightly beaten

Wash and pat dry the squid tubes and cut into thin rings. Put the rings in a flat non-metallic dish and pour the lemon juice over the top. Cover and refrigerate for 15 minutes. Drain and pat dry.

Combine the cornflour, salt, pepper and sugar in a bowl. Fill a deep heavy-based saucepan one-third full of oil and heat to 180°C (350°F), or until a cube of bread dropped in the oil browns in 15 seconds. Dip the squid into the egg white and dust with the salt and pepper mixture, shaking off any excess. Add the squid to the oil in batches and deep-fry for 1–2 minutes, or until golden. Serve immediately.

Serves 8–10

thai chicken cakes

4 eggs, lightly beaten
2 tablespoons finely chopped
   coriander (cilantro) leaves
1 tablespoon fish sauce
2 tablespoons oil
500 g (1 lb 2 oz) minced
   (ground) chicken
3 stems lemon grass, white
   part only, finely chopped
2 garlic cloves, crushed
4 spring onions (scallions),
   chopped

3 tablespoons lime juice
1 large handful coriander
   (cilantro) leaves and stems,
   extra, chopped
2 tablespoons sweet chilli sauce
1 tablespoon fish sauce
1 egg, extra, lightly beaten
125 ml (4 fl oz/$1/2$ cup) coconut
   milk
6 red chillies, seeded and finely
   sliced

Preheat the oven to 200°C (400°F/Gas 6). Lightly grease three 12-hole shallow patty tins. In a bowl combine the eggs, coriander and fish sauce. Heat the oil in a large frying pan over medium heat, add the egg mixture and cook for 2 minutes each side, or until golden. Roll up and shred finely.

Process the chicken, lemon grass, garlic, spring onion, lime juice, extra coriander, sauces, extra egg and coconut milk in a food processor until fine but not smooth. Spoon into the patty tins and top with the shredded omelette. Bake for 15 minutes, or until cooked. Rotate the trays once to ensure the cakes cook through evenly. Serve hot, garnished with chilli.

Makes 36

salt and pepper squid

lounge Late night grooves and low-key lounging with a group of your closest friends require a special kind of sustenance to keep the party going. Throw away the take-out menus and indulge your guests with a grown-up midnight feast. Forget the rule book and let the late hour create a magic all of its own. At this time of night, you can get away with anything.

Late-night lounging is distinct from the cocktail hour in several fundamental ways, aside from the lateness of the hour. While cocktails are about lots of people mingling, lounging is about a small group of friends gathering for some laid-back late-night revelling. Whether you're planning to cater for the post-pub or pre-club crowd, the food should be substantial and the drinks simple and plentiful. Late-night grooves are the inspiration for this type of event and you should think of it as being more like a meal than any of the others. The dishes you serve your guests should work together as well as being delicious on their own and it's a good idea to plan around leaving yourself free to sit and relax with your friends as much as possible. The aim of lounging is not to impress but to create an atmosphere that is sophisticated and relaxed, stimulating and chilled, with food that stimulates the senses while the setting and the ambient music create a feeling of relaxation. There is a definite retro chic aesthetic associated with late-night lounging: think of the fifties — the era of crooners, lounge clubs and hard liquor — as a source of inspiration when it comes to decorating and serving the food. Pull out the hostess trolley, dig out some angular, graphic servingware and give it a modern twist by matching it with cutting-edge food and music. Conjure up that lounging mood and kick back into a spot of cruisy, late-night lounging.

thai fish cakes

500 g (1 lb 2 oz) firm white fish
    fillets, skin removed
1¹/₂ tablespoons red curry paste
55 g (2 oz/¹/₄ cup) sugar
3 tablespoons fish sauce
1 egg

100 g (3¹/₂ oz) snake beans,
    thinly sliced
10 makrut (kaffir lime) leaves,
    finely chopped
oil, for deep-frying
sweet chilli sauce, to serve

Put the fish in a food processor and process until smooth. Add the curry paste, sugar, fish sauce and egg. Process for another 10 seconds, or until combined. Stir in the beans and lime leaves. Shape the mixture into walnut-sized balls, then flatten them into patties.

Fill a wok one-third full of oil and heat to 180°C (350°F), or until a cube of bread dropped in the oil browns in 15 seconds. Cook in batches for 3–5 minutes, turning occasionally. Drain on crumpled paper towels. Serve hot with sweet chilli sauce.

Makes 24

lime prawns

6 tinned sugar canes
48 raw king prawns (shrimp),
    peeled and deveined
125 ml (4 fl oz/1/2 cup) lime juice
lime wedges, to serve

Cut the sugar canes into 5 mm (1/4 inch) thick strips 10 cm (4 inches) long. Thread two prawns onto each sugar cane skewer (you may need to make small cuts in the prawns to make this easier).

Brush the prawns lightly with lime juice and cook in a hot lightly oiled chargrill pan (griddle) for 2–3 minutes each side, or until the prawns are cooked through. Serve with lime wedges.

Makes 24

lime prawns

oysters with pine nuts and bacon

24 fresh oysters on the half shell
2 rindless rashers of bacon
30 g (1 oz) butter
1 small onion, finely chopped
100 g (3$^{1}/_{2}$ oz/1 small bunch)
  rocket (arugula), leaves torn
2 teaspoons Worcestershire
  sauce
2 tablespoons toasted pine nuts,
  roughly chopped

Remove the oysters from their shells, then cover and refrigerate until needed. Wash the shells in hot water and pat dry.

Cook the bacon under a preheated grill (broiler) until crisp. Cool, then break into small shards.

Melt the butter in a frying pan, add the onion and cook, stirring, until soft. Add the rocket and cook until just wilted. Stir in the Worcestershire sauce.

Divide the rocket mixture among the oyster shells, return the oysters to the shells and top with the bacon shards. Scatter the pine nuts over the top and serve warm or cold.

Makes 24

grilled prawns with tequila mayonnaise

4 tablespoons olive oil

2 tablespoons lime juice

24 raw king prawns (shrimp),
    peeled and deveined,
    tails intact

1 tablespoon tequila

160 g (5^3/$_4$ oz/^{2}/$_3$ cup)
    whole-egg mayonnaise

Combine the olive oil and lime juice in a non-metallic bowl and season well. Add the prawns, cover and refrigerate for 1 hour.

Mix the tequila into the mayonnaise, then transfer to a serving dish.

Heat a barbecue hot plate or chargrill pan (griddle) to hot, add the prawns and cook for 1–2 minutes on each side, or until pink and cooked through. Serve with the tequila mayonnaise for dipping.

Makes 24

oysters with pine nuts and bacon

Cute as a button and undeniably ladylike, we defy you to show any restraint when faced with a platter of these burgers.

mini hamburgers

8 burger buns, split in half
(or Turkish bread)
400 g (14 oz) minced (ground)
beef
25 g (1 oz/¼ cup) dry
breadcrumbs
3 French shallots, very finely
chopped
1 tablespoon Dijon mustard
1 tablespoon Worcestershire
sauce
4 tablespoons tomato sauce

olive oil, for pan-frying
100 g (3½ oz) thinly sliced
Cheddar cheese, cut into
24 squares, each 3 cm
(1¼ inches)
24 baby rocket (arugula) leaves,
stems removed and torn into
2.5 cm (1 inch) pieces
½ small red onion, thinly sliced
12 cornichons (baby gherkins),
cut in half

Stamp out rounds from the burger buns using a 4 cm (1½ inch) cutter; you should get 24 from the tops and 24 from the bases. If your buns are quite thick, trim them with a serrated knife after you have cut them.

Combine the beef, breadcrumbs, shallots, mustard, Worcestershire sauce, 1 tablespoon of the tomato sauce and some salt and cracked black pepper in a bowl. Divide the mixture into 24 walnut-sized pieces. With wet hands, shape the pieces into balls, then flatten into patties.

Heat a large heavy-based frying pan with enough oil to just cover the bottom of the pan. Cook the patties over medium heat for 1–2 minutes on each side, or until browned and cooked to your liking.

Top each bun base with a cheese square and grill for 1 minute, or until the cheese is just starting to melt. Lightly grill the bun tops.

Put the patties on the bun bases and top with the remaining tomato sauce, the rocket and onion. Gently press on the bun tops and secure with a cocktail stick stuck through a cornichon half. Serve warm.

Makes 24

mini hamburgers

crispy vermicelli cakes with sesame vegetables

oil, for pan-frying
400 g (14 oz) dried rice
    vermicelli, soaked in boiling
    water for 3 minutes, then
    drained until very dry
2 teaspoons sesame oil
2 carrots, cut into julienne strips

1 red capsicum (pepper),
    cut into julienne strips
2 zucchini (courgettes),
    cut into julienne strips
4 spring onions (scallions),
    cut into julienne strips
1/2–1 tablespoon oyster sauce

Heat the oil in a large heavy-based frying pan over medium heat. Shape tablespoons of the noodles into flat discs, add to the pan in batches and cook for 3 minutes, or until crisp and golden. Drain on paper towels.

Heat the sesame oil in a wok and stir-fry the vegetables for 3 minutes, or until slightly softened. Stir in the oyster sauce and cook for 2 minutes. Spoon the vegetables over the noodle cakes and serve.

Makes about 12

salmon carpaccio with pear, caperberry and cress

200 g (7 oz) salmon fillet
1 pear, cut into julienne strips
4 caperberries, cut into quarters

small handful mustard cress
extra virgin olive oil, for drizzling
2 lemons

Slice the salmon very thinly and divide the slices among 16 small Chinese soup spoons. Top each spoon with a few strips of pear, a caperberry quarter and a few sprigs of mustard cress. Drizzle with some extra virgin olive oil, a squeeze of lemon juice and black pepper.

Makes 16

salmon carpaccio with pear,
caperberry and cress

Using lemon grass stems as skewers allows their fragrance to permeate the chicken and makes a handle for dipping.

chicken and lemon grass skewers

5 stems lemon grass
1 kg (2 lb 4 oz) chicken thigh fillets,
    cut into 2 cm (3/4 inch) cubes
9 French shallots (eschalots), cut in half
3 tablespoons soy sauce
3 tablespoons mirin
2 tablespoons sugar
1 stem lemon grass (white part only),
    extra, finely sliced
1 red chilli, seeded and finely chopped

Trim the leaves off the lemon grass stems. Cut the thicker ends of the stems into 10 cm (4 inch) lengths, then into quarters lengthways. Make a small slit in the centre of each chicken cube and through the shallot pieces, to make threading easier.

Thread alternate pieces of chicken and shallot onto the lemon grass stems, using two pieces of chicken and one piece of shallot for each stem.

Mix together the soy sauce, mirin and sugar.

Cook the skewers in a hot chargrill pan (griddle) or frying pan for about 3–5 minutes. Brush the skewers with half the soy mixture as they cook, turning frequently. Add the sliced lemon grass and chilli to the remaining soy mixture and serve with the skewers, for dipping.

Makes 18

chicken and lemon grass skewers

ratatouille mini pies

3 tablespoons olive oil
1 eggplant (aubergine), diced
1 onion, finely chopped
1 red capsicum (pepper), diced
1 zucchini (courgette), diced
1 tablespoon tomato paste
   (purée)

1 large tomato, chopped
1 teaspoon dried Italian herbs
750 g (1 lb 10 oz) ready-rolled
   shortcrust pastry
1 egg, lightly beaten
ready-made or home-made
   pesto, to serve

Heat 2 tablespoons of the oil in a frying pan and cook the eggplant until golden. Remove. Heat the remaining oil in the pan and cook the onion, capsicum and zucchini for 2 minutes. Stir in the tomato paste, tomato, herbs and eggplant. Cook for 20 minutes, or until reduced. Leave to cool.

Preheat the oven to 180°C (350°F/Gas 4) and put a baking tray in the oven. Lightly grease 24 mini muffin holes.

Roll the pastry thinly and cut out 24 rounds with a 7 cm (2³/4 inch) cutter. Repeat with a 5.5 cm (2¹/4 inch) cutter. Put a large round in each muffin hole and fill with the cooled filling. Dampen the edges of the small rounds and put them on top of the filling to seal the pies. Brush with egg. Put the tin on the hot baking tray and cook for 25 minutes, or until golden. Cool slightly, then remove from the tin. Serve with pesto.

Makes 24

cheese fondue

1 garlic clove, cut in half
3 tablespoons white wine
200 g (7 oz/1 1/2 cups) grated
   Gruyère cheese
185 g (6 1/2 oz/1 1/2 cups) grated
   Cheddar cheese

small mushrooms, cauliflower
   and broccoli florets, and
   crusty bread, to serve

Rub the inside of a fondue dish with the garlic clove, add the white wine to the dish and bring to the boil. Reduce the heat to a simmer, add the Gruyère and Cheddar and stir until the cheeses melt completely. Cook over low heat for 4–5 minutes.

Serve with the mushrooms, cauliflower, broccoli and bread to dip in the fondue, using a skewer or a fork.

Serves 4

cheese fondue

These colourful vegetable shapes are delicious slathered with zesty sour cream and topped with fried leek.

vegetable shapes with sour cream and fried leek

2 x 425 g (15 oz) long, thin orange sweet potatoes, peeled
5 beetroots
125 ml (4 fl oz/$1/2$ cup) sour cream
1 garlic clove, crushed
$1/4$ teaspoon finely grated lime zest
oil, for deep-frying
2 leeks, cut into long, thin strips

Put the sweet potatoes in one large saucepan of water and put the beetroots in another. Bring them to the boil over high heat and simmer, covered, for 30–40 minutes, or until tender, adding more boiling water if it starts to evaporate. Drain separately and set aside until cool enough to handle. Remove the skins from the beetroots and cut them lengthways into 1 cm ($1/2$ inch) slices. Cut the sweet potato into 1 cm ($1/2$ inch) rounds. Using a biscuit cutter, cut the slices and rounds into shapes. Leave to drain on paper towels.

Put the sour cream, garlic and lime zest in a bowl and mix together well. Refrigerate until ready to use.

Fill a deep heavy-based saucepan one-third full of oil and heat to 190°C (375°F), or until a cube of bread dropped in the oil browns in 10 seconds. Tie a few strips of leek into a knot and deep-fry for 10 seconds, or until lightly golden and crisp. Drain on crumpled paper towels and season with salt. Repeat with the remaining leek strips to make 35 knots in total.

To assemble, put a teaspoon of the sour cream mixture on top of each vegetable shape and top with a fried leek knot.

Makes about 35

vegetable shapes with
sour cream and fried leek

baguette with egg, dill pesto and prosciutto

8 thin slices of prosciutto
1 French bread stick, sliced diagonally into 30 pieces
45 g (1½ oz/1 heaped cup) chopped dill
80 g (2¾ oz/½ cup) pine nuts, toasted
2 garlic cloves, crushed

65 g (2¼ oz/⅔ cup) finely grated Parmesan cheese
4 tablespoons virgin olive oil
10 g (¼ oz) butter
7 eggs, lightly beaten
4 tablespoons milk
1 tablespoon light sour cream

Preheat the oven to 200°C (400°F/Gas 6). Put the prosciutto on a baking tray lined with baking paper. Bake for 5 minutes, or until sizzling and crisp. Put the bread on baking trays and bake until golden on both sides.

Put the dill, pine nuts, garlic and Parmesan in a food processor and finely chop. With the motor running, add the oil in a thin stream and process until smooth. Season. Spread the dill pesto over the bread slices.

Heat the butter in a non-stick frying pan over low heat. Add the combined eggs and milk. As the egg begins to set, use a wooden spoon to scrape the base to bring the cooked egg to the surface. Continue for 10 minutes, or until cooked but still creamy. Remove from the heat and stir in the sour cream. Season. Spread the egg on the toasts and top with torn prosciutto.

Makes 30

paprika lamb

18 French-trimmed lamb cutlets
1 tablespoon olive oil
1/4 teaspoon ground cumin
1/2 teaspoon smoked paprika

1 garlic clove, crushed
lemon wedges, to serve

Put the lamb cutlets in a large bowl with the olive oil, cumin, paprika, garlic and a pinch of salt. Mix well, then cover and refrigerate for at least 3 hours, preferably overnight.

Preheat an oiled barbecue hotplate or chargrill pan (griddle) to high and cook the cutlets for 4–6 minutes, turning once. Season with black pepper and serve with the lemon wedges to squeeze over.

Makes 18

paprika lamb

phad thai

100 g (3¹/2 oz) 5 mm (¹/4 inch)
thick dried rice noodles
1 tablespoon vegetable oil
1 egg, lightly beaten
2 teaspoons small dried shrimp
2 teaspoons sugar
2 teaspoons tamarind purée
1 tablespoon fish sauce

2 teaspoons lime juice
¹/4–¹/2 teaspoon chilli powder
90 g (3¹/4 oz/1 cup) bean sprouts
2 teaspoons garlic chives, cut
into 2 cm (³/4 inch) lengths
40 g (1¹/2 oz/¹/4 cup) dry-roasted
peanuts, chopped

Soak the rice noodles in boiling water for 8 minutes, then drain. Heat the oil in a wok over medium heat and cook the egg until firm. Remove from the wok and slice thinly.

Add the dried shrimp and noodles to the wok and stir-fry over high heat for 1 minute, or until the noodles begin to turn golden. Add the sugar, tamarind, fish sauce, lime juice and chilli powder and stir-fry for 1 minute. Stir in the bean sprouts, garlic chives and egg slices, and cook until the bean sprouts wilt.

Spoon into eight small bowls or noodle boxes, sprinkle the peanuts over the top and serve with chopsticks.

Serves 8

chicken san choy bau

1 1/2 tablespoons vegetable oil
1/4 teaspoon sesame oil
3 garlic cloves, crushed
3 teaspoons grated fresh ginger
6 spring onions (scallions), thinly sliced
500 g (1 lb 2 oz) minced (ground) chicken
115 g (4 oz/2/3 cup) drained water chestnuts, finely chopped

90 g (3 1/4 oz/1/3 cup) drained bamboo shoots, finely chopped
3 tablespoons oyster sauce
2 teaspoons soy sauce
3 tablespoons sherry
1 teaspoon sugar
4 small witlof (chicory/Belgian endive) heads, leaves separated
oyster sauce, extra, to serve

Heat the oils in a wok or large frying pan, add the garlic, ginger and half the spring onion and stir-fry over high heat for 1 minute. Add the chicken and cook for 3–4 minutes, or until just cooked, breaking up any lumps.

Add the water chestnuts, bamboo shoots, oyster and soy sauces, sherry, sugar and the remaining spring onion. Cook for 2–3 minutes, or until the liquid thickens a little. Cool slightly, then divide among the witlof leaves (you will need about 2 heaped teaspoons per leaf). Drizzle with oyster sauce and serve immediately.

Makes about 36

phad thai

empanada

250 g (9 oz/1 cup) Italian tomato passata
1 tablespoon pickled jalapeño, chopped, plus 1 tablespoon of juice from the jar
2 tablespoons roughly chopped coriander (cilantro) leaves
1 teaspoon olive oil
1/2 red onion, finely chopped
1 garlic clove, crushed
150 g (51/2 oz) minced (ground) beef
1 teaspoon tomato paste (purée)
1/4 teaspoon ground cumin
1/8 teaspoon sweet paprika
3 sheets ready-rolled shortcrust pastry
1 egg yolk, beaten

Put the passata, pickled jalapeño and juice in a saucepan and cook over medium heat for 5 minutes. Allow to cool, then stir in the coriander.

Heat the oil in a frying pan over medium heat and cook the onion, garlic, beef, tomato paste, cumin and paprika for 3–4 minutes, stirring often to break up the meat. Remove from the heat, season and allow to cool.

Preheat the oven to 180°C (350°F/Gas 4). Using an 8 cm (31/4 inch) cutter, cut 16 rounds from the pastry. Put 1 tablespoon of the beef mixture in the centre of each round and brush around the edge with beaten egg yolk. Fold the pastry over to make a half-moon shape, and press the edges together firmly. Brush the tops with egg yolk and bake for 15–18 minutes. Serve warm with the spicy tomato sauce.

Makes 16

polenta wedges with bocconcini and tomato

1 tablespoon olive oil
250 g (9 oz/1²/₃ cups) polenta
75 g (2¹/₂ oz/³/₄ cup) grated
   Parmesan cheese
2¹/₂ tablespoons ready-made
   or home-made pesto

150 g (5¹/₂ oz) fresh bocconcini
   cheese, thinly sliced
12 cherry tomatoes, cut into
   quarters
1 handful basil, larger leaves
   torn

Grease a 20 x 30 cm (8 x 12 inch) baking tin with the olive oil. Bring 1 litre (35 fl oz/4 cups) of lightly salted water to the boil in a saucepan. Add the polenta in a steady stream, stirring continuously to stop lumps forming. Reduce the heat to very low. Simmer, stirring regularly, for 20–25 minutes, or until the polenta starts to come away from the sides of the pan. Stir in the Parmesan and season well. Spoon the polenta into the baking tray and smooth the top with the back of a wet spoon. Leave for 1 hour, or until set.

Once the polenta has set, carefully tip it out onto a board and cut it into 24 x 5 cm (2 inch) squares, then cut each square into two triangles. Chargrill the polenta in batches on a preheated chargrill pan (griddle) for 2–3 minutes on each side, or until warmed through.

Spread each triangle with 1 teaspoon of the pesto, and top with a slice of bocconcini and a tomato quarter. Season and grill (broil) for 1–2 minutes, or until the cheese just starts to melt. Garnish with basil and serve hot.

Makes 48

empanada

Iced water is the magic ingredient that makes tempura batter so light and crispy, and the finished dish so incredibly addictive.

mixed tempura

12 raw king prawns (shrimp)
1 sheet of nori, cut into 12 thin strips
250 g (9 oz/2 cups) tempura flour or
    plain (all-purpose) flour
500 ml (17 fl oz/2 cups) iced water
2 egg yolks, lightly beaten
oil, for deep-frying
flour, for coating
60 g (2¹/4 oz) broccoli florets
100 g (3¹/2 oz) button mushrooms
1 red capsicum (pepper), cut into thin strips
soy sauce, to serve

Peel and devein the prawns, leaving the tails intact. Cut a little slit in the underside of each prawn (this will prevent them curling) and wrap a piece of nori around the base of the tail.

Sift the flour into a bowl, make a well in the centre and add the iced water and egg yolk. Stir with chopsticks until just combined. The batter should be slightly lumpy.

Fill a deep heavy-based saucepan one-third full of oil and heat to 180°C (350°F), or until a cube of bread dropped in the oil browns in 15 seconds.

Dip the prawns in flour to coat, shake off any excess, then dip in the batter. Add the prawns to the oil in batches and cook until crisp and light golden. Drain on paper towels. Repeat with the broccoli, mushrooms and capsicum. Serve the tempura immediately with soy sauce for dipping.

Makes about 30

mixed tempura

gulab jamun

100 g (3½ oz/1 cup) powdered milk
50 g (1¾ oz/⅓ cup) blanched almonds, ground
155 g (5½ oz/1¼ cups) plain (all-purpose) flour
1 teaspoon baking powder
½ teaspoon ground cardamom
30 g (1 oz) butter, chopped
60 g (2¼ oz/¼ cup) plain yoghurt
220 g (8 oz/1 cup) sugar
a few drops of rose water
oil, for deep-frying

Sift the dry ingredients into a bowl. Rub in the butter with your fingertips until the mixture resembles fine breadcrumbs. Make a well, then add the yoghurt and 2–3 tablespoons of water. Mix with a flat-bladed knife to form a soft dough. Shape into small balls, then cover with a damp cloth.

Put the sugar and 375 ml (13 fl oz/1½ cups) of water in a saucepan and stir until the sugar dissolves. Simmer for 5 minutes. Stir in the rose water.

Fill a heavy-based saucepan one-third full of oil and heat to 180°C (350°F), or until a cube of bread browns in 15 seconds. Deep-fry the dough balls in batches until deep brown. Don't cook them too quickly or they won't cook through. They should puff up a little. Drain in a sieve set over a bowl. Put the warm balls in a deep bowl and pour the syrup over the top. Leave to soak and cool until still slightly warm. Drain and serve piled in a bowl.

Makes about 35

chocolate coffee cups

200 g (7 oz/1¹/₃ cups) dark
 chocolate melts (buttons)
20 foil confectionery cups
1 tablespoon cream

50 g (1³/₄ oz/¹/₃ cup) chopped
 white chocolate
1 tablespoon coffee liqueur
20 chocolate coffee beans

Put the chocolate melts in a heatproof bowl. Bring a saucepan of water to the boil, remove from the heat and sit the bowl over the pan, making sure the bowl does not touch the water. Stir occasionally until the chocolate has melted. Cool slightly.

Working with one foil cup at a time, put 1 teaspoon of melted chocolate in each. Use a small paintbrush to coat the inside with chocolate, making sure it is thick and there are no gaps. Turn the cups upside down on a wire rack and leave until firm. Return the remaining chocolate to the bowl over steaming water for later use.

Combine the cream, white chocolate and coffee liqueur in a heatproof bowl. Stir over a saucepan of simmering water until smooth. Cool slightly, then spoon into the chocolate cups. Press a coffee bean into each cup. Allow to set. Re-melt the reserved chocolate. Spoon it over the filling and tap to level, then leave to set.

Makes 20

Lounge parties are the perfect place to indulge in a bit of retro chic — for that personal touch, add your own messages.

chinese fortune cookies

3 egg whites
60 g (2^{1}/$_{4}$ oz/^{1}/$_{2}$ cup) icing (confectioners') sugar, sifted
45 g (1^{1}/$_{2}$ oz) butter, melted
60 g (2^{1}/$_{4}$ oz/^{1}/$_{2}$ cup) plain (all-purpose) flour

Put the egg whites in a bowl and whisk until just frothy. Add the icing sugar and butter and stir until smooth. Add the flour and mix until smooth. Set aside for 15 minutes.

Preheat the oven to 180°C (350°F/Gas 4). Line a baking tray with baking paper. Draw three 8 cm (3^{1}/$_{4}$ inch) circles on the paper, then turn the baking paper over.

Using a flat-bladed knife, spread 1^1/$_2$ level teaspoons of the cookie mixture over each circle. Bake for 4–5 minutes, or until slightly brown around the edges.

Working quickly, remove the cookies from the baking trays by sliding a flat-bladed knife under each one. Put a folded written message inside each cookie.

Fold the cookies in half, then in half again over a blunt-edged object. Allow to cool on a wire rack and cook the remaining mixture in the same way. Make only three cookies at a time, otherwise they will harden too quickly and break when folding. If this happens, return the tray to the oven and warm them through.

Makes 20

chinese fortune cookies

rich chocolate truffles

185 ml (6 fl oz/3/4 cup) thick
    (double/heavy) cream
400 g (14 oz) good-quality
    dark chocolate, grated

70 g (21/2 oz) butter, chopped
2 tablespoons orange liqueur
dark cocoa powder, for coating

Put the cream in a small saucepan and bring to the boil. Remove from the heat and stir in the chocolate until it has completely melted. Add the butter and stir until melted. Stir in the orange liqueur. Transfer to a bowl, cover and refrigerate for several hours or overnight, or until the mixture is firm enough to roll.

Quickly roll 2 teaspoons of the mixture into balls, and refrigerate until firm. Roll the balls in the cocoa, shake off any excess and return to the refrigerator. Serve at room temperature.

Makes about 40

rum and raisin truffles

60 g (2¹/4 oz/¹/2 cup) raisins,
finely chopped
3 tablespoons dark rum
200 g (7 oz) chocolate-coated
wheatmeal (wholemeal)
biscuits, crushed
60 g (2¹/4 oz/¹/3 cup) soft
brown sugar
1 teaspoon ground cinnamon

50 g (1³/4 oz/¹/2 cup) pecans,
finely chopped
3 tablespoons cream
250 g (9 oz/1²/3 cups) chopped
good-quality dark chocolate
90 g (3¹/4 oz/¹/4 cup) golden
syrup
125 g (4¹/2 oz/1 cup) pecans,
extra, finely ground

Combine the raisins and rum in a small bowl and marinate for 1 hour. Put the crushed biscuits, sugar, cinnamon and chopped pecans in a large bowl and mix together well.

Put the cream, chocolate and golden syrup in a saucepan and stir over low heat until melted. Add to the biscuit mixture, stir in the rum and raisins and mix to combine. Refrigerate until the mixture is just firm enough to roll into balls.

Roll 2 teaspoons of the mixture into balls, then roll the balls in the ground pecans. Refrigerate until firm.

Makes about 60

Densely chewy yet delicate, these chocolate cups with a filling of caramel and cream will send your tastebuds into orbit.

chocolate caramel cups

150 g (5 1/2 oz/1 cup) dark chocolate melts (buttons)
18 small foil confectionery cups
80 g (2 3/4 oz) chocolate fudge caramel bar, chopped
3 tablespoons cream
50 g (1 3/4 oz/1/3 cup) white chocolate melts (buttons)

Put the dark chocolate melts in a small heatproof bowl. Bring a small saucepan of water to the boil and remove from the heat. Sit the bowl over the pan, making sure the bowl does not touch the water. Stir occasionally until the chocolate has melted.

Using a small new paintbrush, brush a thin layer of chocolate inside the foil cases. Stand the cases upside down on a wire rack to set. Return the remaining chocolate to the bowl over steaming water for later use.

Combine the chopped fudge bar and cream in a small saucepan and stir over low heat until the fudge has melted and the mixture is smooth. Transfer to a bowl and leave until just starting to set, then spoon into each foil cup, leaving about 3 mm ($\frac{1}{8}$ inch) of space at the top.

Re-melt the reserved dark chocolate, spoon it into the caramel cases and tap to level. Leave to set.

When the dark chocolate has set, melt the white chocolate in the same way as the dark chocolate. Spoon it into a small paper piping bag and drizzle patterns over the cups, or just spoon a small amount on each. Leave to set.

Makes 18

index

Published in 2010 by Murdoch Books Pty Limited

Murdoch Books Australia
Pier 8/9, 23 Hickson Road
Millers Point NSW 2000
Phone: +61 (0)2 8220 2000
Fax: +61 (0)2 8220 2558
www.murdochbooks.com.au

Murdoch Books UK Limited
Erico House, 6th Floor
93–99 Upper Richmond Road
Putney, London SW15 2TG
Phone: +44 (0)20 8785 5995
Fax: +44 (0)20 8785 5985
www.murdochbooks.co.uk

Chief Executive: Juliet Rogers

Publisher: Lynn Lewis
Senior Designer: Heather Menzies
Design Layout: Handpress Graphics
Editor: Justine Harding
Editorial Coordinator: Liz Malcolm
Production: Joan Beal

National Library of Australia Cataloguing-in-Publication entry
Title: Fingerfood. ISBN: 978-1-74196-945-0 (pbk.)
Series: New chubbie. Notes: Includes index. Subjects: Appetizers. Dewey Number: 641.812

Text, photography and design copyright © Murdoch Books Pty Limited, 2010.
All rights reserved. No part of this publication may be reproduced, stored in a retrieval system or transmitted in any
form or by any means, electronic, mechanical, photocopying, recording or otherwise, without the prior written
permission of the publisher.

Printed by 1010 Printing International.
PRINTED IN CHINA

IMPORTANT: Those who might be at risk from the effects of salmonella poisoning (the elderly, pregnant women, young
children and those suffering from immune deficiency diseases) should consult their doctor with any concerns about
eating raw eggs.

OVEN GUIDE: You may find cooking times vary depending on the oven you are using. For fan-forced ovens, as a
general rule, set the oven temperature to 20°C (35°F) lower than indicated in the recipe.